Smart Engagement

Why, What, Who and How

John Aston

astoneco management

john.aston@astoneco.com

Alan Knight

Social Impact Partners

alan@socialimpactpartners.com

First published in 2014 by Dō Sustainability
87 Lonsdale Road, Oxford OX2 7ET, UK
Copyright © 2014 John Aston and Alan Knight

The moral right of the author has been asserted.

ISBN 978-1-910174-19-7 (eBook-ePub)
ISBN 978-1-910174-20-3 (eBook-PDF)
ISBN 978-1-910174-18-0 (Paperback)

A catalogue record for this title is available from the British Library.
Dō Sustainability strives for net positive social and environmental impact. See our sustainability policy at **www.dosustainability.com**.

Page design and typesetting by Alison Rayner
Cover by Becky Chilcott

For further information on Dō Sustainability, visit our website:
www.dosustainability.com

DōShorts

Dō Sustainability is the publisher of **DōShorts**: short, high-value ebooks that distil sustainability best practice and business insights for busy, results-driven professionals. Each DōShort can be read in 90 minutes.

New and forthcoming DōShorts – stay up to date

We publish 3 to 5 new DōShorts each month. The best way to keep up to date? Sign up to our short, monthly newsletter. Go to **www.dosustainability.com/newsletter** to sign up to the Dō Newsletter. Some of our latest and forthcoming titles include:

- *Leadership for Sustainability and Change*   Cynthia Scott & Tammy Esteves
- *The Social Licence to Operate: Your Management Framework for Complex Times*   Leeora Black
- *Building a Sustainable Supply Chain*   Gareth Kane
- *Management Systems for Sustainability: How to Successfully Connect Strategy and Action*   Phil Cumming
- *Understanding Integrated Reporting: The Concise Guide to Integrated Thinking and the Future of Corporate Reporting*   Carol Adams
- *Corporate Sustainability in India: A Practical Guide for Multinationals*   Caroline Twigg
- *Networks for Sustainability: Harnessing People Power to Deliver Your Goals*   Sarah Holloway
- *Making Sustainability Matter: How To Make Materiality Drive Profit, Strategy and Communications*   Dwayne Baraka

- *Creating a Sustainable Brand: A Guide to Growing the Sustainability Top Line* Henk Campher
- *Cultivating System Change: A Practitioner's Companion* Anna Birney
- *How Much Energy Does Your Building Use* Liz Reason
- *Lobbying for Good: How Business Advocacy Can Accelerate the Delivery of a Sustainable Economy* Paul Monaghan & Philip Monaghan
- *Creating Employee Champions: How to Drive Business Success Through Sustainability Engagement Training* Joanna M. Sullivan

Subscriptions

In addition to individual sales of our ebooks, we now offer subscriptions. Access 60+ ebooks for the price of 5 with a personal subscription to our full e-library. Institutional subscriptions are also available for your staff or students. Visit **www.dosustainability.com/books/subscriptions** or email **veruschka@dosustainability.com**

Write for us, or suggest a DōShort

Please visit **www.dosustainability.com** for our full publishing programme. If you don't find what you need, write for us! Or suggest a DōShort on our website. We look forward to hearing from you.

Abstract

SMART BUSINESSES IN THE 21ST CENTURY will be those that are best at adapting to changing societal concerns, expectations, risks and opportunities and that know how to generate sustainable outcomes. To be one of these smart businesses you need *Smart Engagement*. While many companies talk a lot about stakeholder engagement, few do it in a way that genuinely contributes to business success. In many cases, companies engage the wrong people on the wrong issues at the wrong time; they take too long or not long enough planning, and too much or not enough time doing it; they slide into PR-mode and try to manage rather than engage; and they undermine relationships by creating expectations that will rarely be met or by investing in making decisions and activities few people want. This is not Smart Engagement. While there are a number of guidelines on engagement out there, there is little consensus on best practice and on how engagement should be integrated into core business. *Smart Engagement* is based on years of experience in the field and distils the best from current research and practice guidance. What sets it apart is its straightforward, no-nonsense approach. It focuses on results and creating value; it is not an abstract process guideline.

About the Authors

JOHN ASTON has 20 years' experience in strategy, and project design, management and communication, in countries including Ireland, UK, France, Austria, Slovakia, Romania, Bulgaria, Turkey, South Africa, Zimbabwe, Yemen and Canada. His areas of expertise include natural resources, energy and infrastructure projects for the private sector, World Bank or national governments, and include design, implementation, environmental management, social responsibility and capacity building. He has been an engineering consultant, a vice president of a junior mining company, and a member of the technical committee that created the international stakeholder engagement standard AA1000SES (2011). Since 2006, John manages his own company in project co-creation in support of sustainable results. He is a visiting lecturer at a number of universities. He graduated in civil and environmental engineering in Ireland and France, is a Chartered European Engineer and has a Masters in environmental management from Imperial College, London.

ALAN KNIGHT has over 25 years of experience advising corporations, governments and civil society on sustainability issues, specialising in corporate responsibility, stakeholder engagement, monitoring and evaluation, and sustainability assurance. Alan has worked with many major international corporations in the utility, manufacturing, oil and gas, mining, aeronautics, chemical, pulp and paper and financial sectors, and has written extensively on a range of related standards and sustainability subjects. He has been a member of numerous boards and advisory and technical committees related to management systems, auditing and assurance, environmental and social performance evaluation and reporting. Alan has been a Senior Fellow at AccountAbility in London, a Vice President with ICF International in Toronto and Washington DC, and an Assistant Professor at McGill University in Montreal. He has published a number of books, studies, monographs and articles on a wide range of sustainability issues. Alan has a PhD from the University of Alberta, Canada, has qualified as a certified environmental auditor and is an accredited impact investment advisor.

....

Acknowledgments

WE WOULD LIKE TO ACKNOWLEDGE that the stakeholder engagement processes presented here have drawn on best practices and extensive experience that we gained through our work with colleagues, communities, clients and partners. We thank each one of them.

We would also like to thank those who have reviewed all or parts of this manuscript and shared their comments and ideas with us, including Penny Walker, Meredith Sassoon, Andreea Savu and Edmond McLoughney.

Contents

CHAPTER 1

Introduction

Who is this book for?

THE EASIEST WAY TO START would be to say that this book is for everybody.

While this is a broad claim it is one that we feel is warranted since our basic premise is that engagement is a fundamental management process.

However, as a starting point, we would suggest that this book is most important for those people who participate in making decisions, both strategic and operational. This is most likely to include:

- those in senior management and boards (whether public, private or third sector), or those advising strategic decision-making;

- those who enable, make and implement operational decisions;

- internal and external stakeholders who want more sustainable decisions and outcomes; and

- those involved in designing and implementing engagement as process facilitators or engagement practitioners.

Also, while organisations in all sectors need to engage stakeholders, it is our experience that some feel a more compelling need than others.

These include:

- the high social and environmental impact sectors – mining, oil & gas, infrastructure, manufacturing;

- the consumer-facing sectors – consumer goods, service organisations, social services;

- the 'at risk' sectors – financial institutions with exposure to the two sectors above;

- the regulated sectors – such as government agencies, charities, supply chains (with contractual requirements), businesses with covenants in loan agreements (e.g. for IFC Standards, Equator Principles); and

- the policy-makers – government departments and agencies, local government, international governmental institutions.

This book will also be especially useful to organisations that wish to fulfil requirements of various codes and standards such as:

- the GRI reporting guidelines;

- the International Integrated Reporting Framework;

- the UN Global Compact;

- the Equator Principles;

- the Principles for Responsible Investment;

- ISO26000;

- AA1000.

Finally, this book is also for those interested in or already committed to sustainable development. For it is not just about engagement.

Smart Engagement is about engagement *that leads to* successful and sustainable outcomes for all concerned.

What is Smart Engagement?

This book then is about how to integrate *Smart Engagement* into the planning, execution and management of the decisions and activities undertaken to run our organisations successfully and sustainably. It is the first in a series of books that trace the road towards *Smart Business*.

For us, a *Smart Business* is one that delivers results (outcomes) that are not only financially and technically successful but also socially and environmentally acceptable and sustainable. Engaging stakeholders in a smart way is fundamental to achieving this.

Organisations typically engage for one of two reasons: 1) they're in trouble, or 2) they need innovation to improve something.

Trouble can come from various directions. It can be:

- financial pressure due to losing market share or not winning contracts;

- legal pressure as a result of social or environmental infractions;

- pressure from the public or civil society groups who object to something that is or is not being done, produced, proposed.

Case study 1: Water management company

A large water management company had a contract to provide potable water to households in a large South American city.

As part of their agreement they were also to provide water to a number of neighbourhoods where the homes did not already have access to piped water. For a range of technical reasons they were not able to meet the targets for access by new households. The local government received many complaints. The water management company was put on notice that its contract was at risk of not being renewed. At the same time they were bidding on a new contract in the same area. The water company realised that many of the complaints were based on a lack of information and misinformation. They accepted that this was their fault. They immediately initiated a comprehensive engagement program with households, local government and other stakeholders. They explained their situation, received suggestions and ideas, and began to build relationships and partnerships to resolve the problems. The new ideas and partnerships were built into their bid for renewal as well as for the new contract. They won both.

Note: This book uses real case studies to illustrate specific aspects of the engagement process. Names have not been assigned to keep the focus on the challenge rather than the organisation involved.

Stakeholders can assist you in, or prevent you from, achieving your objectives. They influence the effectiveness and efficiency of your operations, and the attainment of your goals. The absence of effective dialogue can lead to conflicts that may delay or stop your progress and can be costly to correct.

Organisations often begin to engage when in trouble; but once they realise that engagement is effective in achieving better outcomes they begin to do it as a matter of course. *Smart Engagement* includes doing engagement as a matter of course, of making it part of core business practice.

Three prime motivators of engagement are:

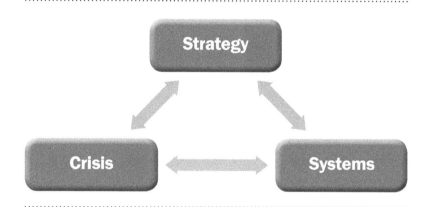

- **Crisis** – you've got a problem you need to fix; you engage to fix it; the result can be either a strategic or an operational fix; many organisations start and stop here; they never move on; they think of engagement as a crisis tool;

- **Systems** – others say 'hey, engagement helped us out with a problem, maybe if we use it more systematically we'll have fewer problems'; this is usually an operational fix; and

- **Strategy** – the big boss twigs and says 'well, engagement has really helped us do what we do better, perhaps it can also help us figure out what to do next in a more sustainable and successful way'; the result is a strategic fix and a move towards *Smart Business*.

Smart Businesses don't wait until they are under pressure or in trouble before they start engaging. They see that engaging with stakeholders can be an extraordinary source of new ideas and innovation that can give them a competitive edge; they see that building relationships and partnerships can improve company profile and reputation, and provide access to opportunities that might otherwise not have been available to them; they see that engaging with knowledgeable stakeholders can give them a better understanding of risk and of ways to mitigate and manage risk; they see that stakeholder support is essential to gaining permits and licences to operate.

One other point: you can do crisis engagement without doing systematic or strategic engagement, but even if you engage systematically and strategically you may still have crises to deal with – although, one hopes, far less often. In reality, not only will engaging early result in getting in trouble less often, but you will also be much better equipped to respond more quickly and effectively when required; and you might even be surprised by your stakeholders working to support you during a given situation rather than working against you.

Why are we saying this? Because engagement is not just a curative. Engagement needs to happen early. Trust is very hard to build in a crisis. It takes more time and costs more money to be reactive than proactive. Don't wait until there is a problem to engage. By engaging early and integrating engagement into an organisation's core functions, you stay ahead of the curve.

Let's look at a few reasons for this:

- Relationships are built on intangibles such as trust, mutual respect and understanding. These take time to develop and evolve.

- A proactive approach means you will be better equipped to predict potential issues, risks and opportunities, to influence perceptions, set a constructive tone of dialogue, and be able to generate sustainable solutions.

- Early engagement will signal to stakeholders that their views and well-being are important and will be listened to.

- As most crisis engagements have shown, relationships are much harder to build if significant tensions exist. The absence of established relationships and channels of communication puts organisations at an immediate disadvantage and significantly increases risks.

- Due to negative perceptions, it becomes harder to reach out to third parties such as government agencies or NGOs. Even if these latter stakeholders are not particularly affected, they might be reluctant to assist in solving a problem due to the reputational risk of being associated with the issues in question.

- In a world where electronic communication is so prevalent and quick (email, YouTube, Facebook, Twitter, Instagram, etc.), mistakes, or perceived mistakes, are public before you know it.

Case study 2: Getting in early

A local natural resource company belonging to a large international group was becoming more and more alarmed at the level of concern and misinformation it was witnessing in local media and in interactions with local authorities, local landowners and concerned

---

local citizens. The international group advised local management not to engage until the legal permitting process required it. At one point, as problems with local community and authorities started to manifest, the top management of the local group sought independent advice from an engagement professional. Building rapport quickly, the engagement professional was invited to site and, after examining the risks and opportunities posed by the proposed project, met some of the local leaders on an informal basis. Realising that the main cause of the impending local conflict was fear of the 'what ifs', the engagement facilitator convened informal meetings between the local leaders and the local management. Together they outlined the arguments why prior and informed consultation would be in everyone's interest. This was then sent to the international group on an internal letterhead and provided the foundation for the organisation to agree to convene an open and transparent engagement process.

In short, *Smart Engagement* is engagement that is strategic and systematic rather than reactive; it is engagement driven by the need to generate sustainable outcomes and not just financial or technical success. It is a core function of the organisation and conducted in such a way that stakeholders are integrated into strategic and operational decision-making. Once integrated as a core function, *Smart Engagement* enables you to achieve more in a shorter period of time, with fewer resources and less stress.

FIGURE 1. Get your head out of the sand: the case for Smart

In summary, we define *Smart Engagement* as an engagement process designed and implemented with stakeholders that results in accepted, accountable and sustainable outputs and outcomes.

In this short book, we provide the framework and tools to get you started; the foundation to inspire, adapt and innovate; and a path to meet the societal challenges facing organisations today.

We have tried to make *Smart Engagement* easy to read, easy to understand and easy to follow.

CHAPTER 2

The *Smart Engagement* Framework

Creating value

THE GOAL IS *SMART BUSINESS*. *Smart Engagement* is a fundamental function of, and the starting point for, *Smart Business*. As we said in the Introduction, smart businesses in the 21st century will be those that are best at adapting to changing societal concerns, expectations, risks and opportunities and that know how to generate sustainable outcomes.

FIGURE 2. The building blocks for achieving Smart Business.

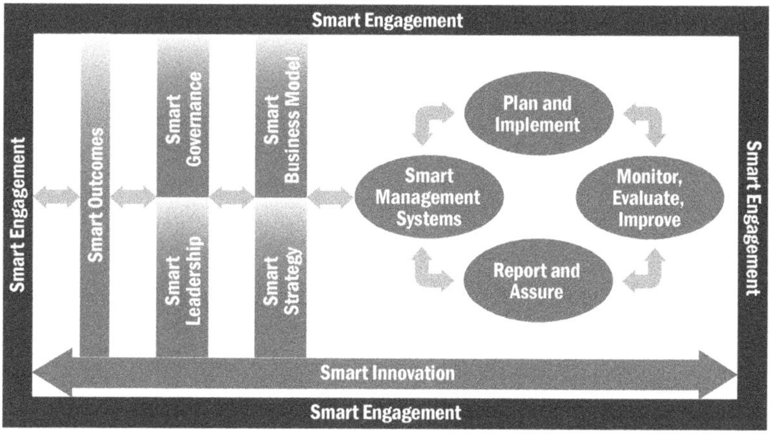

Smart Engagement works best and creates most value in the context of an organisation whose strategy is to generate *Smart Outcomes*. The decisions and actions resulting from *Smart Engagement* generate *Smart Outcomes*. To achieve these outcomes requires the right leadership, governance, strategy, business model, management systems and innovation. All of these need to be *Smart* as well.

Smart Outcomes

Smart Outcomes are the value created or protected as a result of the outputs of an organisation. Outputs are the immediate result of an organisation's decisions, which is to say its activities, products and services.

Smart Outcomes must be technically feasible, economically viable, and socially and environmentally acceptable and sustainable, and can be measured by their contribution to financial, social, natural, manufactured and human capitals.

Smart Leadership and Governance

Good leadership is about ensuring good decisions are made and inspiring others to perform well. It is also about identifying whom to work with. *Smart Leadership* adds two fundamental attributes: an understanding and commitment to accountably engage with stakeholders, and an understanding and commitment to identify and deliver *Smart Outcomes*.

Smart Strategy and Business Model

A *Smart Strategy* is a plan to achieve *Smart Outcomes*.

A *Smart Business Model* is how we structure our business across the value chain to deliver our *Smart Strategy*.

Smart Management Systems

Smart Management Systems support *Smart Strategies* and *Smart Business Models*. They enable us to plan tactically and implement our strategic plan within the structure of our *Smart Business Model*.

Smart Innovation

Innovation is the continual improvement of solutions in response to needs and expectations. *Smart Innovation* is the creation of solutions that continuously improve our outcomes.

The framework

The four components of the *Smart Engagement* framework link the purpose, scope and stakeholders of engagement (the 'Why', the 'What' and the 'Who') to relevant engagement processes (the 'How'). The 'How', like any good process, also includes a step to identify ways to improve.

....

FIGURE 3. The Smart Engagement framework.

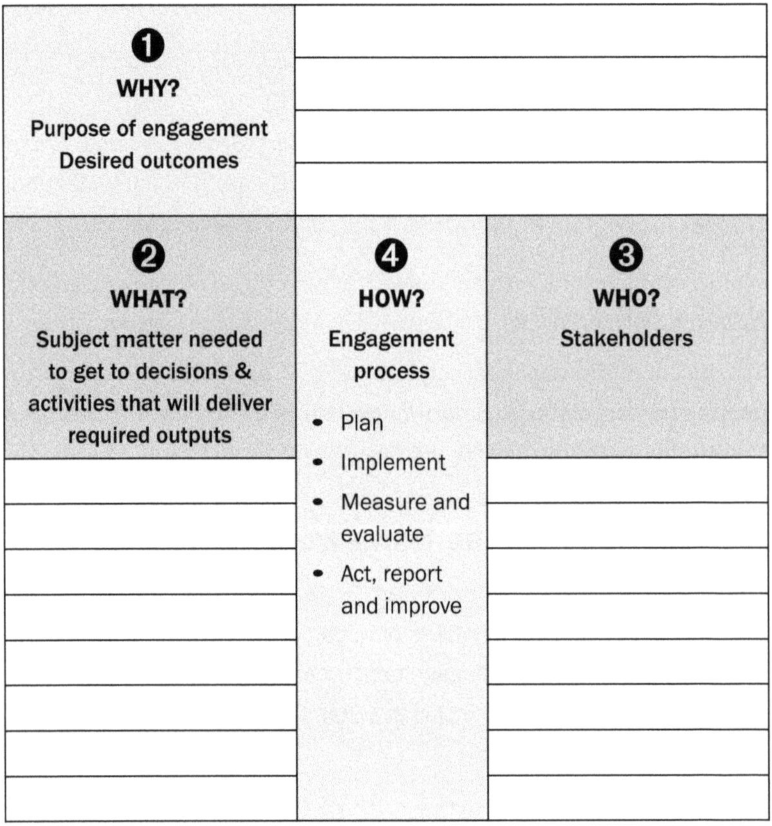

❶ **WHY?** Purpose of engagement Desired outcomes		
❷ **WHAT?** Subject matter needed to get to decisions & activities that will deliver required outputs	**❹** **HOW?** Engagement process • Plan • Implement • Measure and evaluate • Act, report and improve	**❸** **WHO?** Stakeholders

....

The process of creating clarity around the 'Why', 'What' and 'Who' is iterative and underpins Smart Engagement.

Component 1: Why

Defining and agreeing the purpose of engagement is essential.

We look at two broad categories of purpose: 1) strategic and 2) operational. A strategic purpose is usually about doing something new or different to create a desired outcome. An operational purpose usually has to do with operationalizing strategic decisions or doing better what you already do.

While we have distinguished between strategic and operational purpose, it is often the case that an engagement will include both. Once you start discussing a new strategy it is sometimes hard not to want to jump into operational issues. This is fine. There is no need to conduct strategic and operational engagements independently (although you may wish to since they often require different knowledge and skills).

The example below demonstrates both the differences and similarities.

	EXAMPLE
What is the **strategic** challenge?	Our competitors are beating us on price because they are outsourcing back-office functions to low-wage economies. But we value our employees and don't want to have to make anybody redundant.
WHY: The **strategic** purpose?	To find a way to remain competitive without outsourcing to low-wage economies.
What is the desired future state or **outcome**?	We are competitive while maintaining local employment.
What is the desired **output**?	A decision on which strategy to follow.

	EXAMPLE
What is the **operational** challenge?	How can we achieve the 'no low-wage economy' strategy?
WHY: The **operational** purpose?	To find ways to implement the 'no low-wage economy' strategy.
What are the desired **outputs**?	The changes to products, services and processes needed to achieve the 'no low-wage economy' strategy.

Component 2: What

As the purpose is identified and agreed, you need to define what you are going to engage on to help achieve the purpose. In other words the scope of engagement needs to be defined. The scope usually includes a consideration of three things: the subject matter, the boundaries and the time horizons.

If the purpose is strategic, the scope will include the various strategic options. If it is operational, the scope will include the various ways to operationalize the strategic decision.

And of course, the scope of any engagement will be developed or adjusted by the stakeholders participating in the engagement.

Component 3: Who

The 'Who' is about everybody who has a stake in the 'Why' and the 'What'. The engagement process also includes the initiators and the implementers.

The people who initiate an engagement are the people who start the whole thing off and who bring together the necessary people and groups needed to make it happen. The initiators typically draft a first statement of purpose and begin to assemble the necessary resources.

The initiators then help mobilise the people or groups who can implement the engagement. They may come from a single organisation or from a partnership. The implementers should strive to occupy a neutral position and should not have a direct stake in the outcomes and outputs of the engagement. They must not only manage the process but also manage real, potential or perceived conflicts of interest.

The stakeholders of the engagement are those people or groups who have a stake in the outputs and outcomes of the engagement (the 'Why' and the 'What'), whether they choose to participate or not. These will be the people, groups or organisations who are impacted by or have an impact on the outputs and outcomes.

It is important that legitimate stakeholders are not left out as this can lead to problems down the road. You may well find that once an engagement is started the participants identify other stakeholders who should be involved, or that new stakeholders pop up. The process should enable their inclusion at the appropriate level to ensure Smart Outcomes.

The example below shows how the purpose, the scope and the stakeholders are connected, as well as to the decisions that result from engagement.

	EXAMPLE
WHY: The **strategic** purpose	To find a way to remain competitive without outsourcing to low-wage economies.
WHAT: The scope	
Subject matter	Strategic options, e.g.: • Should/could we increase productivity of back office – better IT, more training, streamlined processes, etc.? • Could we compete on quality not price – move to the premium end of market? • Would we benefit from a centralised back office for all operations? • Other?
Boundaries	All European operations.
Time horizon	Begin to implement changes in six months.
WHO: The stakeholders	People with a stake in the 'Why' or 'What' are part of the process to define the above, and the design and implementation of the engagement process that leads to the Output and Outcome – e.g. employees, managers, owners, customers, authorities, etc.
Decision (**output** of the engagement)	One of the agreed options (e.g. compete on quality not price).

	EXAMPLE
WHY: The operational purpose?	To find ways to implement the 'no low-wage economy' strategy.
WHAT: The scope	
Subject matter	Operational options for chosen strategy (e.g. compete on quality not price) • What new product and service opportunities exist at the premium end of the market? • What product and service design expectations are there at the premium end of market? • What technical, economic, social and environmental expectations do our customers have of products and services? • What products and services would need to be dropped? • Other?
Boundaries	All European operations.
Time horizon	Begin to implement changes in six months.
WHO: The stakeholders	Employees, managers, owners, customers, authorities, etc.
Decisions (outputs of the engagement)	• Mandate to redefine product and service portfolio based on recommendations of what to add and drop. • Mandate to define design spec for portfolio based on agreed expectations. • Mandate to conduct R&D for new and redesigned products and services.

Component 4: How

The 'How' is the process stuff. It is all about planning, implementing, monitoring, evaluating, reporting and improving. To simplify this, a standard Deming-like plan–do–check–act cycle is useful.

But perhaps the most important thing about the 'How' is the need to understand that there are different levels of engagement and different methods of engagement for each level. There is no one-size-fits-all engagement process. And it is not advisable to move to higher levels of engagement by bypassing lower ones.

We use two levels of pre-engagement: tracking and informing; and four levels of engagement: consulting, including, collaborating and empowering. There are then a number of methods that work best at each level.

Success depends on enabling a process whereby interested stakeholders can address material issues using the level of engagement and methods they are comfortable with, and which are most effective and efficient in developing Smart Outcomes.

But remember that real life doesn't always go according to plan. We often say that engagement is like walking a tight rope. Through engagement: you know the starting point; you know the desired end point; you have a plan: the rope. But staying on the rope is a skilled balancing act that requires constant adjustment.

These four components will be explained in more depth in Chapters 3 to 6.

Smart Engagement and accountability

Smart Engagement is also an accountability mechanism.

> *Accountability is acknowledging, assuming responsibility for and being transparent about the impacts of your policies, decisions, actions, products, services and associated performance. It obliges an organisation to involve stakeholders in identifying, understanding and responding to sustainability issues and concerns, and to report, explain and be answerable to stakeholders for decisions, actions and performance.* AA1000APS, 2008

Accountability is achieved when the engagement outputs and outcomes are technically feasible, economically viable, and socially and environmentally acceptable.

....

FIGURE 4. Smart Engagement enables accountable and socially inclusive outputs and outcomes.

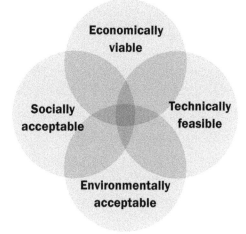

....

CHAPTER 3

Why Engage?

HERE WE LOOK MORE CLOSELY at the strategic and operational purpose of *Smart Engagement*.

Common strategic and operational reasons to engage include:

- To enable better understanding of and response to risk, opportunity and change;
- To inform the development of, ensure understanding of, and receive feedback on policies and strategies;
- To build trust, social capital and social inclusion;
- To make strategic decisions collaboratively and so be supported by a stronger team;
- To minimise misunderstandings and delays due to poor communication;
- To mobilise commitment and motivation for change;
- To pool resources such as knowledge, people, money and technology;
- To solve problems, reach objectives or implement improvements;
- To enable input to planning, testing, design, permitting and team building.

Strategic challenges

Strategy is usually defined as the methods or plans chosen to get to a desired future state, that is, to the desired outcomes. Strategic challenges often, though not always, have to do with aspects of the external environment that have to be addressed to achieve the desired outcomes. The external environment refers to those things that an organisation typically does not control but that can have an impact on its success.

Organisations typically call these aspects 'risks and opportunities' and list them under categories such as:

- **Political** – 'will the laws governing what we do change, is there a legal requirement to engage?'

- **Macro-economic** – 'will we fall into recession, will interest rates go up?'

- **Social capital** – 'will consumer or community groups attack us, will we lose our social licence to operate?'

- **Natural capital** – 'will raw material inputs become scarce and more expensive, will the cost of waste disposal go up?'

- **Suppliers and relationships** – 'will suppliers maintain quality of supply, are supplier decisions and actions sustainable, will key relationships disappear or turn sour?'

- **Competitors and demand** – 'will our competitors introduce innovations that affect demand for our products and services?'

Case study 3: Gold mining company

A gold mining company obtained a licence to exploit a gold deposit during a period of national privatisation. Before receiving a permit to operate it began investing money, designing and developing the project and convincing shareholders how successful they were going to be. At the same time, and without their knowledge, civil society was becoming more and more convinced that the company had obtained their licence in a corrupt fashion and were not the kind of partners they wanted to see in their country. Consequently, they went on the attack and portrayed the company as the symbol of all that was wrong in the country. As a response, company lawyers made countless presentations to the company's board, and in court, to show how legal everything was. The company spent millions on local and national PR campaigns. Civil society challenged the permitting process at every step, often focusing on the decisions of the authorities and not just those of the company. Even if the company won many cases in court, a permit to operate has still not been granted 10 years on.

Even though an organisation may have little control over these aspects, you still need to understand them; and you may be able to influence them. This is where *Smart Engagement* comes in.

A successful organisation tracks, analyses, and where possible, tries to anticipate and participate in change. There are a number of ways to do this: you can watch the news every night and read the *Economist*; you can commission research or read the stuff commissioned by somebody else;

or you can, from the beginning, talk with the people involved, in other words, you can engage your stakeholders. Engagement doesn't mean you don't have to do the other stuff. It simply means you do everything you can to make informed, sustainable decisions.

It also allows us to get beyond factual evidence and to understand why people act and take the positions they do. As behavioural economists, sociologists and others have shown us over the last several years, people don't always act rationally. Where there is uncertainty or a lack of evidence or trust, people act on values, intuitions, assumptions and beliefs. Making decisions solely on the basis of factual evidence in a marketplace motivated by behaviour can get you into trouble. So we need to engage to understand other people's values, intuitions, assumptions and beliefs. To be socially acceptable, outputs and outcomes need to be based on this understanding.

This is not to say that organisations are rational and stakeholders irrational. Far from it. It is often the other way round. What it means is that we need to make strategic decisions based on an understanding of shared values, needs and interests. *Smart Engagement* gives us access to this understanding.

Taking this into consideration, when trying to nail down the strategic purpose, it is often helpful to ask the following two questions:

1. Do we fully understand the risks and opportunities in our environ-ment(s)?

2. Will engaging with relevant stakeholders help us to better understand the risks and opportunities and how to respond to them (i.e. develop a better strategy)?

If the answer to the first question is yes, then you are either already engaging well with your stakeholders or you are like the ostrich in Figure 1.

If the answer to the second question is yes, then you should engage. If it is no, which is possible, then there is no reason to engage.

One final point: a strategy is basically the articulation of a direction an organisation should follow. What this means in practice is that all decisions must be consistent with and measured against these strategies. So a good place to start may be:

- What decisions need to be made?; and then,

- Will engagement help make a better decision?

Case study 4: Large construction company

A large construction company has a legal obligation to engage stakeholders. They are aware that legislation requiring this includes:

- Strategic Environmental Assessments (SEAs) & Environmental Impact Assessments (EIAs);

- some international conventions that can impact their business, e.g. the Aarhus and the Espoo Conventions;

- commitment to the Equator Principles.

The company's engagement is managed by their PR department and supported by their legal team. Their engagement activities

---

are limited to the legal requirement to disclose information to, and conduct public meetings with, stakeholders.

Over a number of projects the public consultation meetings required by the law were adversarial in nature. The company recognised that there was a high level of mistrust between them and the external stakeholders.

Following this experience and some related enquiries, the company has realised that the legally required engagement programs are not sufficient to enable an organisation to mitigate business risks, nor do they address the need for internal and external capacity building for engagement.

Further, the company has become concerned that they are not meeting the 'prior and informed consent' criteria of their financing organisations (e.g. Equator Principles).

They have gone back to the drawing board to consider stakeholder engagement more strategically.

Operational challenges

Operations are about producing the outputs (products, services, processes, by-products) that a strategy says are needed in order to achieve strategic outcomes (desired future state).

Operational challenges have to do with how well you plan, implement, monitor, review and report on the production of these outputs. For example, do you have the right people, the right inputs, the right processes and so on to generate products and services that are technically feasible, economically viable and socially and environmentally acceptable? These are the challenges linked to the means of production over which you have control. Operational challenges and solutions are increasingly subject to stakeholder expectations. They are not a purely internal issue. Also, both internal and external stakeholders represent a valuable source of ideas for operational improvement.

Businesses typically capture these operational aspects under categories such as:

- **Financial** – 'how well are we managing our finances?'

- **Reputational** – 'how well are we managing our image brand and trust?'

- **Human capital** – 'how well are we managing people?'

- **Intellectual capital** – 'how well are we managing intellectual property rights?'

- **Occupational health and safety** – 'how well are we managing health and safety in the workplace?'

- **Manufactured capital** – 'how well are we managing facilities and equipment?'

- **Natural capital** – 'how well are we managing waste, spills, resource use, etc.?'

- **Quality** – 'how well are we managing on-time, quality product and service delivery?'

Using engagement to inform everyday planning, execution and management of operations makes a lot of sense. New perspectives bring new ideas. Old hands know existing procedures and equipment inside out and know where improvements can be made.

Engaging external stakeholders on operational issues takes nerve and it takes trust. You are sharing information on your organisation that you may feel is confidential or that you feel may not present you in a positive light. You are admitting that you may not have all the answers; and you are committing yourself to listening and, perhaps more importantly, to acting on what you hear.

The good news is that engagement not only takes trust but, when done well, builds trust that adds not only organisational but also social value. Trust is rewarded. Trust is built around how we think, act and talk. It enhances reputation. It builds community. It builds staff morale. It builds teams.

The questions that need to be asked for operational challenges are similar to those asked for strategic challenges:

1. Are all of the operational risks and opportunities fully understood?

2. Will engagement help understand them better and help develop innovative ways to improve and create more social and organisational value?

If the answer to the first question is no, then engagement should be undertaken.

If the answer to the second question is yes, then engagement should be undertaken.

Often engagement on operational issues is first considered by management because there is a problem in operations that needs to be addressed. You therefore ask yourself:

- What operational problems do I have?

- Will engagement help develop a better solution to these problems?

Case study 5: Packaged goods company

A large packaged goods company has 40,000 suppliers around the world. As a first step, it evaluated suppliers against a set of international environmental protection and ethical labour practice standards. It then engaged with all suppliers to develop and implement a set of rigorous responsible sourcing standards that set out how the company and its suppliers work together. The company now maintains regular dialogue with these suppliers. Because of this, suppliers make frequent suggestions and recommendations on ways to improve product quality and operational efficiency. All recommendations are evaluated, and if they make good sustainability and business sense they are acted on. Working in partnership with suppliers has made a significant contribution to the improved quality of material inputs and to the social responsibility of operations.

Trust is enhanced when stakeholders – internal and external – are involved in decision-making rather than just consultations (the latter being when stakeholders are asked for their views but are not involved in decision-making). This is no small order. Most managers and professionals have not been prepared to work in this way. They are trained to accept responsibility, to assume authority and to make decisions – even if these decisions, because of the impact they may have on stakeholders, would benefit significantly from stakeholder participation and would be more broadly accepted. To involve stakeholders is not to abdicate responsibility. It is the accountable exercise of responsibility. We find time and time again that involving stakeholders in decision-making results in better decisions and outcomes.

So, to summarise this first component: always identify why engagement is needed. Without a clearly defined purpose, engagement usually won't achieve much and may even set you back.

Go to worksheet 1: Why? The purpose of the engagement –
www.smartbusinessacademy.org

A clarifying note

Be sure to distinguish between the decisions that need to be made and the information needed to support making those decisions. For example, it is sometimes difficult to make strategic decisions without taking operational considerations into view. How can you decide whether looking to increase the productivity of the back office is a better choice than a shift to compete on quality rather than price if you don't know the cost implications, the skill and knowledge requirements or the technical feasibility? You need the operational information in the engagement – and therefore to include stakeholders with operational expertise – but the only decision you are going to make is the strategic one: 'what strategic option will we choose to address the increasing competition from those who are outsourcing back-office operations to low-wage countries?' Operational decisions are not being made at this point so the engagement does not have an operational purpose. But it informs operations and operations inform it.

On the other hand, it may be efficient to design an engagement process that serves both a strategic and operational purpose. For example, you may have a situation in which you have a failing product line. You need to make a strategic decision about whether to drop it or try to revive it. If the strategic decision is to revive it, it may then make sense to continue the engagement and to explore the best ways to revive it.

Outcomes and outputs

You should always try to describe your strategic purpose in relation to the **outcome** – or future state – you want to achieve. So, as in the example above, if your **purpose** is to find a way 'to remain competitive without outsourcing to low-wage economies', you are doing this because the **outcome** you want to achieve is 'to be competitive while maintaining local employment'.

A strategic engagement also has **outputs**. In this example, the **output** is the **decision** for example, on whether or not to 'compete on quality not price'. Outputs are chosen because they are considered the best way to achieve a desired outcome.

CHAPTER 4

What To Engage On

HERE WE LOOK MORE CLOSELY at how we define what we will engage on: the subject matter, the boundaries and the time horizon.

Subject matter

The 'Why' and the 'What', the purpose and the scope, of *Smart Engagement* are very closely aligned.

In the example we used above, the strategic purpose was 'to find a way to remain competitive without outsourcing to low-wage economies'. The subject matter would include all of the strategic options that need to be considered, such as: an increase in the productivity of the back office – better IT, more training, streamlined processes; to compete on quality not price – move to premium end of market; or to centralise back office for all operations. It might also include the operational considerations for each strategic option, the expectations of the premium market and so on. In other words, information on any subject that will help you make a better strategic decision. During an engagement new options and subjects usually come up. Give them space. You are looking for ideas. You may have to come back to them later if you need to do more research.

If the purpose of the engagement (the 'Why') is to find a solution to an operational problem, such as how 'to find ways to implement the "no low-wage economy" strategy', the subject matter will include such things as the 'operational options for the chosen strategy' – for example, to compete on quality not price; new product and service opportunities at premium end of market; product and service design expectations at premium end of market; technical, economic, social and environmental expectations of products and services; and products and services that would need to be dropped. Once again, include any subject that will help make better decisions and always be open to new ideas.

What to engage on can be as varied as why to engage. There is no short crib sheet of the six or eight things you need to engage on so that you can tick the box and say you have engaged. This is where you open Pandora's box and see what comes out. It is where you assemble the raw materials for innovation and creativity. In reality, a Smart Engagement process enables the stakeholders to develop the criteria for what to engage on and select what stays on the table and what drops off. Being open-minded before being rigorously analytical is a great advantage.

Boundaries

The scope should also consider the boundaries of what is going to be engaged on. Boundaries to be considered include:

- What organisations or parts of the organisation to include – the whole of the organisation or a single business unit, function or operation?

- What geographical regions to include – worldwide operations or those of a single country or region? and

- What activities, products or services to include – everything the organisation produces or does, a single line of products or a single product or service?

In the example used above, the decision was taken to look at a strategic challenge in relation to an organisation's European operations. Labour issues are typically more geographically focused. But if the issue had been a more global concern such as climate change, stakeholders may have decided to look for a strategy for global operations. Or if there was an operational challenge related to the late delivery or high failure rate of a certain product, the scope might be best limited to that product line.

It also needs to be emphasised that engagement is not something done only by a select few functions such as CSR, HR or Communications. If the people actually responsible for the strategic and operational decisions are not actively involved in the engagement, it is likely to have almost no traction with other stakeholders and therefore be a waste of everyone's time.

Whether we've called it stakeholder engagement or not, building relationships and engaging with people has been around for a long time and been used by many parts of the organisation. If you work in a CSR, communication or sustainability function you should support the people in the other functions, and importantly, promote and enable knowledge and experience sharing. Engagement boundaries, however, may be defined by the part of the organisation most responsible for the challenge or opportunity in question. It may be an engagement on investor relations or brand management, for example.

Some common functions that use engagement

- ☐ Board engagement
- ☐ Investor relations
- ☐ Strategic planning
- ☐ Policy development
- ☐ Change management
- ☐ Brand management
- ☐ Partnership creation
- ☐ Compliance
- ☐ Operations
- ☐ Risk management
- ☐ Environment, health & safety
- ☐ Conflict resolution
- ☐ HR
- ☐ CSR and sustainability

- ☐ External affairs
- ☐ Communications
- ☐ Public relations
- ☐ Marketing
- ☐ Permitting
- ☐ Community relations
- ☐ Project management
- ☐ Event management
- ☐ Crisis management
- ☐ Team meetings
- ☐ Land access
- ☐ Permitting
- ☐ Procurement

But remember that, regardless of the part of the organisation you are engaging on, *Smart Engagement* results must be technically feasible, economically viable and social and environmentally acceptable. It therefore makes a lot of sense for people in different parts of the organisation to work together, share ideas and ideally develop a common organisational approach.

Case study 6: Privatised compliance management company

A provincial government in Canada decided to privatise the management and delivery of regulatory compliance associated with a number of pieces of equipment and product safety legislation. The privatised compliance management company was also to have a public safety advocacy role. When establishing the governance and organisational structure for the new organisation they recognised that government relations, partnerships and public engagement would be a large part of the new company's mode of operation. They, therefore, established a C-Suite that included a chief officer in charge of stakeholder engagement. This has allowed the company to have, from start-up, a common approach to engagement supported by company-wide systems and processes.

Time horizons

Stakeholders need to decide whether the problem you are solving or the opportunity you are trying to identify is long, short or medium term. This brings focus, saves time and avoids confusion.

The decisions on all aspects of the scope will greatly benefit from the involvement of stakeholders in defining the time horizons. This doesn't mean that the initiator does not have a starting proposition. There should be one. But it is good practice, as you move up the 'level of engagement' ladder (see levels of engagement below), to engage on your propositions about scope and to either validate or adjust them based on the substantiated views of stakeholders.

More on outputs

You should rarely, if ever, have an engagement without outputs. If you do you are risking wasting people's time. Engagement outputs are the ideas, perceptions and expectations, recommendations, decisions and actions coming out of the engagement. Depending on the level of engagement you may also need to have the participants validate the outputs.

The outputs link back to the outcome the engagement serves. So if, for example, the desired outcome is greater acceptance of certain wood products in the marketplace, the strategic output might turn out to be a recommendation that only wood products from certified sustainably managed forests be used in the furniture manufacture.

In the example above, the output of the operational engagement might turn out to be a set of decisions that provided the mandate for the organisation to redefine its product and service portfolio based on recommendations of what to add and drop; to define a design specification for a new product portfolio based on agreed expectations; and to conduct R&D for new and redesigned products and services.

Go to worksheet 2: What? The scope of the engagement –
www.smartbusinessacademy.org

One final comment: in reality, defining the scope is an iterative process. It will most probably have to be adjusted based on the views of stakeholders during the engagement. In fact, the 'Why', the 'What' and the 'Who' tend to become clearer and more grounded in reality as the engagement process progresses.

CHAPTER 5

Who To Engage With

THIS CHAPTER LOOKS MORE CLOSELY at who is involved in *Smart Engagement.*

Know your place

First you need to orient yourself.

When you engage you need to understand how to locate the relationship between you and other stakeholders. In the old days, organisations assumed they were in the driver's seat. They owned the universe. Stakeholders were a part of their universe and had to be 'managed'. You fed them what was needed to keep them quiet, complacent or cooperative, and went on with your business.

FIGURE 5. Business as the universe.

FIGURE 6. Stakeholders as the universe.

These days this relationship needs to be flipped on its head. We now acknowledge that the organisation is not the universe but just another satellite in it; the universe is society as a whole and the organisation's stakeholders are a subset of society. This configuration of relationships makes it clear that the organisation is accountable to its stakeholders within the broader context of society as a whole. The distinction between society and stakeholders is important here as no one organisation can hold itself accountable to everyone in society. Stakeholders are different from society as a whole because they have a stake in the business. They have a stake because of its impacts on them or their impacts on it.

The other bit of orientation we need to be aware of is that stakeholders are not just about 'us and them'. You need to think and plan in terms of three key relationship types.

1. The relationship between an organisation and its stakeholders: the impacts of one on the other and expectations concerning each other's behaviour.

2. The relationships between stakeholders: how they view things differently from one another and have different interests and concerns.

3. The relationships and motivations that exist within your organis-ation.

FIGURE 7. Relationship types.

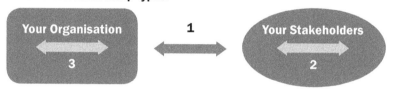

Initiators and implementers

As we mentioned above, the 'Who' is about everybody who has a stake in the 'Why' and the 'What'. The engagement process also includes the initiators and the implementers.

The initiators:

- provide the drive and motivation to engage;

- help bring together the people and groups needed to make it happen;

- typically draft a preliminary statement of purpose; and

- begin to assemble the necessary resources.

Given that an organisation is part of the larger universe and not the universe itself, organisations need to recognise that they may not always be the ones to initiate an engagement. We often assume that this will come from within a single organisation: 'it's our company, we'll decide who to engage with, what to engage on, and why'. While this can be the case for internal engagement, for external engagement it is not.

For example, if an advisory committee made up of independent experts decides to engage on a certain strategic challenge, they are part of the initiating group. Or perhaps you have a bad relationship with the community within which you operate, or wish to operate. There is little communication between your organisation and the community. They then discover that you are planning to open a new facility nearby. They establish a community organisation and convene an engagement to talk about your plans. They even invite you. It's all about your plans. You're there. But they initiate it. You don't.

This may sound threatening but it doesn't have to be. Broadening of the initiating group of the engagement can often also broaden the resource base for the engagement. It also provides a platform to significantly improve relationships and the quality of conversations among stakeholders.

The implementers manage the engagement process – the planning, implementing and reporting. They may come from a single organisation or from a partnership and may not have a direct stake in the outcomes and outputs of the engagement.

The implementers typically receive their initial mandate from the initiators.

Those involved in driving and implementing an engagement may change during the engagement process if stakeholders agree that it will be beneficial to the achievement of the purpose of the engagement.

So, for example, while your organisation may initiate an engagement, over time, and with stakeholder involvement, the purpose may evolve and be revised collaboratively. This can bring new energy and drive to the engagement.

Case study 7: Building a motorway

During the construction of a motorway, where the client was the State and the contractor a reputable construction company, a source for fill for the base of a section of the motorway became unattainable. This led to contractual difficulties and the State resolved this by 'giving' the construction company a quarry site and asking them to get on with it. On the engineering and geological maps this site looked good and the company sent in their equipment. In reality the site was overlooking a village with the nearest house just 100 meters away. Neither the government nor the company undertook local engagement on the matter, despite the fact that part of the finances for the project was coming from EU funds.

Once the villagers started to inquire what the bulldozers were doing there, they quickly found that the company had no permits for its new quarry. You can imagine what dust and noise on a 24-hour basis added to the mix. However, as the overall outcome of the quarry was the motorway – a project already decided by government and underway – the community focused on improving the situation rather than trying to block the bulldozers. Therefore, they organised themselves into a group with the mission to ensure that responsible environmental management was enforced and that, once the work was finished, the site would be responsibly restored. Encountering a lack of openness to dialogue from the constructor and the authorities, the group then focused on communicating the situation through photo and video documentation distributed on YouTube. As a consequence, the company started to work more closely with the community for a more sustainable outcome. The result was improved dust and noise control; and, once the motorway was complete, the restoration of the hill, as agreed among stakeholders. The restoration included 3000 trucks of soil put back on a landscaped hill and the planting of 8000 trees.

Identify stakeholders

Identifying and mapping stakeholders involves identifying the people or groups who have a stake in the 'Why' (purpose) and the 'What' (scope) of the engagement. To start with, it is often useful to identify groups or organisations rather than individuals.

Case study 8: European mining company

A new company purchased mining rights to a gold mine in Eastern Europe. In this region, companies (and many other forms of organisations including government, NGOs, UN bodies and other international organisations) historically tended to only engage directly with the local mayor and other relevant elected officials. The new company has found that this does not work. From a practical business risk perspective, it doesn't make sense to build a long-term business with a mayor who is in office for a limited time period and with a limited mandate, and who may have existing and conflicting commitments to those who helped him get elected (party bosses, local interest groups, personal interests). It proved much more beneficial to engage with a broad range of groups who could represent a range of needs, values and interests and who could deliver a balanced result, rather than specific individuals who could skew the results due to private interests.

The people who need to be engaged tend to come from three general groups of stakeholders: open society or 'the third sector', the public sector and the private sector. An example of the types of stakeholders within these groups is presented in Table 1.

TABLE 1. Types of stakeholders

Society – third sector	Public sector	Private sector
• Civil society – e.g. NGOs, CBOs, action groups, etc. • Faith-based organisations • Educational institutions • Disadvantaged groups – e.g. unemployed, disabled • Special interest groups – e.g. retirees, students, parents, teachers, land owners, consumers	• Politicians – local, regional, national • Civil service • Government agencies • Regulatory authorities – e.g. environment, health and safety, labour • Public services – e.g. healthcare, police, fire fighters, social services • State-owned enterprises	• Businesses – big, medium, small – local, regional, multinational • Management • Communication staff • Projects & operations • Environment, health and safety • Procurement & finance • Land access • Consultants & contractors • Security • Corporate • Shareholders • Professional associations – e.g. doctors, dentists, lawyers • Trade associations & unions

As previously noted, not all engagements have to include everybody. Some issues only impact people in one or two of these general groups. But also as previously noted, it is important for risk mitigation and opportunity development not to leave out stakeholders that should be at the table. As Figure 8 demonstrates, the three groups often have areas where they overlap as well as areas where there is no overlap at all. This gives us seven potential zones of decision ownership or interest. To make it easier to identify which stakeholders need to be involved in the engagement, it is useful to first understand who 'owns' or needs to 'own' the decisions and actions that are the outputs of the engagement. It is then also useful to know who needs to be involved because of their stake or interest in the subject matter.

....

FIGURE 8. Zones of decision ownership.

....

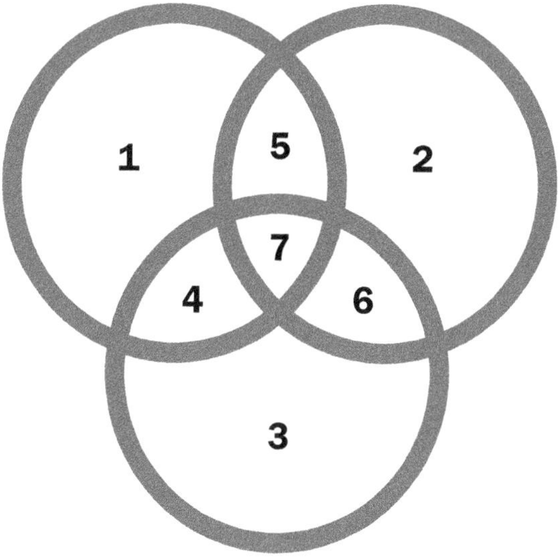

- Zone 1 refers to decisions that the private sector owns, for example, if a company has enough allocated financial capital to afford a certain investment, and if this investment makes sense to them.

- Zone 2 refers to decisions that society owns, such as safety standards for their children.

- Zone 3 refers to decisions that the public sector owns, such as whether or not the law is correctly applied.

- Zone 4 refers to decisions that both the private and public sector own, such as the legal aspects of project permitting.

- Zone 5 refers to decisions that both the private sector and society own, such as night noise levels near a factory.

- Zone 6 refers to the decisions that both the public sector and society own, such as the use of tax money.

- Zone 7 refers to decisions that all three parties own, such as the development of natural resources.

The goal of stakeholder identification and selection is to make sure we have the right stakeholders participating, that is, those who have an interest and a stake in the engagement because they will be impacted by or can have an impact on the issues and concerns that are behind the purpose and scope of the engagement and the decisions that need to be made.

Go to worksheet 3: Who? The stakeholders you engage –
www.smartbusinessacademy.org

Case study 9: Lottery company

A company won the right to manage a national lottery because of their strong commitment to stakeholder engagement. Once they began operations and after an initial survey of stakeholders and their concerns, they found that there were a lot of distinct stakeholder groups with different and distinct issues and concerns. There were the regulators and affiliated companies (the ones who decided who to give the lottery profits away to) who were interested in efficient operations, legal compliance and the fair distribution of profits; there were the stores that sold the lottery tickets who were interested in technology, marketing support and the surveillance of sale to minors; and there were the lottery ticket buyers who were interested in support gambling addiction, fair play and winner protection. In recognition of the different interests and the decisions that the different groups had a stake in, the company decided to set up an advisory council for each distinct set of stakeholders. The work of all of these groups was fed into a single strategic stakeholder advisory council that advised senior management and the board.

A good way to help identify which stakeholders, and therefore which zone the decision belongs in, is to assess whether they have any of the following types of relationship with the underlying issues and concerns and the decisions that will be made.

- **Dependency** – are they dependent on you or are you dependent on them to address this challenge?

- **Responsibility** – do you have obligations to them or do they have obligations to you? These obligations could be legal, commercial, operational or ethical.

- **Tension** – are they putting pressure on you or do they feel you are putting pressure on them? The pressure could be for financial, economic, social or environmental reasons.

- **Influence** – do they have influence on you and your organisation or do you need to influence them? The influence might be because you respect and listen to each other or it could be because they can influence the marketplace or other stakeholders for or against you.

- **Diverse perspectives** – what other people might have different views that can lead to a new understanding that may not otherwise occur? This group may also include those who, through regulation, custom, culture or reputation, can legitimately claim to represent the interests of the voiceless such as future generations and the environment.

If an individual or group has one or more of these types of relationship, they have a stake.

Go to worksheet 4: What? Who? Nature of relationship – www.smartbusinessacademy.org

The initiators of the engagement often do an initial stakeholder identification before they pass things on to the implementers. While realistically this may be where you start, it is important to progress to a more systematic approach.

Case study 10: Economic think-tank

A small UK-based economic think-tank received a research grant to develop a set of common material issues for a highly visible industry sector. They won the grant based on a proposal whose approach included a comprehensive stakeholder engagement process. At the start of the research project the three members of the research team individually generated lists of who the potential stakeholders might be. They then got together, shared and challenged each list against a set of relevancy criteria. This resulted in a consolidated list that was quite a bit different than the individual lists. They then shared the preliminary draft list with the industry association that was funding them. Once again new suggestions were made and existing inclusions questioned. At the end of this process they thought they had a pretty good list. They started putting names to the groups and organisations on their list and then started calling potential participants. They shared information on the scope of their project and on their initial list of stakeholders and asked for suggestions. In most cases this simply resulted in suggestions about who might be the best person to represent an organisation or group on the list. But in a few important conversations new groups were identified that, at the end of the day, enriched the engagement considerably. Another key result was that when the first engagement took place all participants had already been engaged to ask for their input and so there was a high level of buy-in from the start.

Also, we must avoid:

- engaging only with organised groups we know to be friendly, and

- not engaging with those who may not be as friendly.

Profile and prioritise stakeholders

Profiling stakeholders is useful for a number of reasons:

- to understand their interests and concerns – to not waste people's time and resources, it is important to know what their interests and concerns are and what is most material to them;

- to understand their capacity and willingness to engage – so that everyone can participate equally and without resource constraints; and

- to understand their existing attitudes and relationships – to avoid getting unknowingly caught up in other people's battles and have their issues hijack the engagement.

You can start by gathering some basic data on each stakeholder group or organisation. You can choose how sophisticated you want to be here. You may want to set up a stakeholder database. You may want to enter stakeholders into your CRM software. You may just want to keep a few notes on each and not get too fancy. Or you may even just want to use the list of characteristics as an aide-memoire as you review and discuss each stakeholder group. The key point is that you need to know who should be at the table and what their values, needs and interests are. A great way to waste time is to go into an engagement knowing little about who is in the room and what their material issues are.

So you should consider gathering the following kinds of information:

- stakeholder group – e.g. civil society, government, consumer, etc.;

- level of impact of the issue on each group;

- level of influence on the success of the engagement;

- knowledge of the issues – level of expertise;

- current position on the issues;

- relationships between stakeholders – e.g. close or distant, formal or informal, positive or negative;

- level of independence – are there dependencies between the other stakeholders in any way;

- willingness to engage;

- cultural context and perspectives – for example, gender, ethnicity, religion, disability;

- capacity to engage (e.g. language barriers, IT literacy, accessibility needs, willingness to talk openly in public, resources, knowledge, etc.).

Understanding not only the stakeholder group but also the individual(s) who will represent the group can significantly improve the engagement process. So it is helpful to profile the individuals as well. You can do this easily in a simple table.

Go to worksheet 5: Stakeholder profiles –
www.smartbusinessacademy.org

One question often asked is 'how much attention does each stakeholder group deserve or require?' In reality it is not practical, and usually not necessary, to engage with all stakeholder groups at the same level all of the time. This is why it is useful to prioritise them. This will help determine the appropriate level to engage at.

Prioritising is a way of clustering stakeholders. One way to do this is by comparing the level of impact on stakeholders to the level of impact that stakeholders can have.

Typically stakeholders are located on a four-box graph as shown in Figure 9. The box the stakeholder group lands in helps determine what level they need to be engaged at.

....

FIGURE 9. Prioritising stakeholders by impact.

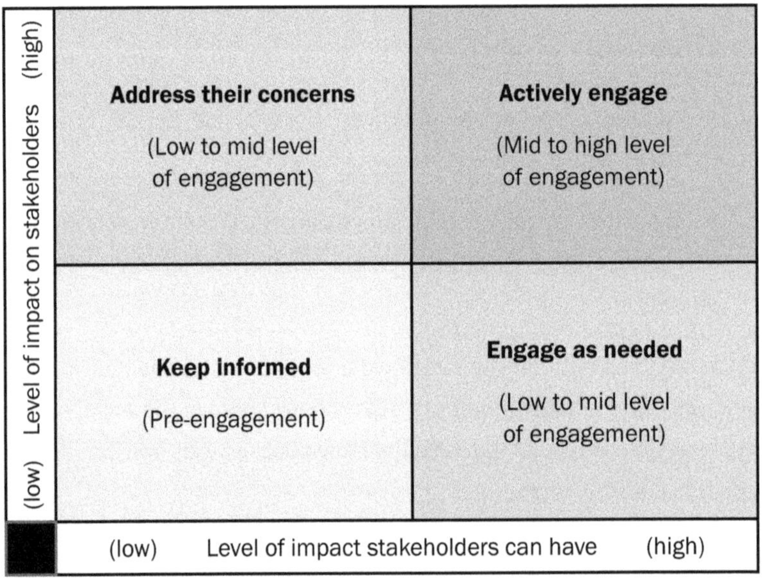

Level of impact on stakeholders (high) / (low)

Address their concerns	Actively engage
(Low to mid level of engagement)	(Mid to high level of engagement)
Keep informed	Engage as needed
(Pre-engagement)	(Low to mid level of engagement)

(low)   Level of impact stakeholders can have   (high)

....

Remember that different stakeholders will have various and sometimes competing positions, interests and needs. For example, community interests may include varying levels of support for the positive impacts of a project (employment or business opportunities), as well as concern for its negative impacts (pollution or social disruption). Therefore, what is positive to one group of stakeholders can appear negative to another. Being aware of stakeholder positions and interests will make it easier to understand and successfully engage with them.

Also, some stakeholders will belong to organised groups whose purpose is to represent particular positions or interests. Others may not be organised and may not have an agreed position – especially acute with respect to vulnerable or disempowered groups. Profiling and prioritising can help identify these latter groups and ensure that the methods of engagement chosen give them a voice.

Attributes, skills and knowledge

Making *Smart Engagement* a reality requires a combination of the right attributes and the right skills and knowledge. Who needs all these attributes, skills and knowledge? Certainly anybody who is responsible for a high-level, multi-stakeholder engagement process should have pretty much the whole package. But remember that engagements often have shared ownership and are the responsibility of a team of collaborators. In such a case you may not have the full package in a single individual but you should try to make sure that you find everything you need in the team.

Also, not all engagements are high-level, multi-stakeholder events. What you need to do is make sure that you have all of the relevant aptitudes, skills and knowledge you need for the required level and method of engagement.

In the best of all possible worlds, participants would also share the aptitudes and the knowledge base. It is often a good idea to share with participants the expectations around aptitudes and knowledge and to build capacity where it is most needed. Stakeholder profiling can help you identify where capacity gaps exist. This capacity building does take time and resources but tends to pay off in the long term.

Here's the full package:

Attributes

Personal behaviour

- integrity;

- respect;

- open-mindedness;

- responsiveness;

- inclusiveness;

- creativity;

- ability to actively listen;

- ability to focus on solutions;

- ability to communicate clearly.

Credibility

- ability to earn and secure trust;

- ability to relate to and be accepted by all stakeholders;

- commitment to accountability and transparency.

Skills

Project management and analysis
- ability to plan and implement a complex process on time;

- ability to access and manage the necessary resources, including information;

- ability to facilitate, to capture the key inputs, messages, insights and outputs and to examine and interpret them in relation to the desired outcomes;

- ability to facilitate and negotiate consensus or agreement; or acknowledge where this is not possible;

- ability to balance engagement dynamics;

- ability to adjust, adapt and change process during the engagement;

- ability to see where more time is needed and to secure this time;

- ability to motivate others to be constructive, creative and innovative.

Communication
- ability to communicate effectively.

Knowledge

Engagement techniques
- knowledge of relevant levels and methods of engagement;

- knowledge of engagement risks and mitigation techniques;

- knowledge of stakeholder identification, profiling and prioritising.

Issues knowledge

- knowledge of the organisations involved;

- knowledge of the specific issues and background to needed decisions that are the subject of the engagement;

- knowledge of the political, social, cultural and environmental context;

- knowledge of the industry sector, including peers and benchmarks;

- knowledge of the stakeholders involved and their perspectives.

External professional practitioners

An organisation might find that it cannot or should not assemble the engagement facilitation team in-house. For example, if an organisation is engaging because it is under pressure from external stakeholders, somebody from within the organisation may not be accepted to run the engagement process. Levels of trust, impartiality and independence may be questioned. In such cases it may be useful to engage an independent, professional engagement practitioner. Engaging a credible, professional practitioner may also make the organisation's senior management a little more comfortable.

Note, however, that once anyone is engaged there will always be a sense that this person or organisation is somewhat biased towards the engaging organisation. This needs to be acknowledged and accounted for. In all cases, it is strongly recommended that the external practitioner values, and is seen to value, all parties of an engagement and not just the client. This not only ensures level playing fields but also contributes to a more sustainable solution. Transparency and accountability are essential to make this a practicable proposition.

A professional *Smart Engagement* leader should have the full package. But even professionals may come as a team. That's quite common. In such a case you should make sure that the team brings everything you need to the table.

Case study 11: Large consumer goods company

A large consumer goods company had been producing a product for years that some felt presented a health risk. In fact, a campaigning NGO was established specifically to challenge the product and the company with the aim of having the product removed from the market. The company did not want to remove the product from the market. In spite of the concerns expressed about health risks the product was one of their biggest sellers. They tried to engage with the NGO but the NGO would not speak to them. They adopted voluntary codes for marketing the product responsibly and did research to assess the health risk claims. Still the campaigning organisation would not engage. They were having an impact in the market. The consumer goods company decided that they could not engage the NGO on their own and so hired a professional practitioner. While the professional practitioner was not able to broker engagement between the company and the campaigning organisation he was able to establish an independent multi-stakeholder group to consider issues associated with the product category rather that the specific product of one company. Due to the independence of the process and the credibility of the professionals managing the process, the campaigning NGO agreed to participate.

Build capacity

A critical part of *Smart Engagement* is building internal and external capacity to engage. Stakeholders who feel empowered (informed, consulted, included, partnered with and with a good engagement skill set) contribute more effectively than those who feel the cards are stacked against them. This is worth investing in.

In order to ensure everyone's time is well used and outputs are acted on, resource and capacity building support is often needed not only for the engagement process itself but also for the implementation of the results of the engagement. It is natural that stakeholders want to see a return on their investment in time and effort. They want to see results.

Engagements are likely to involve people with very different levels of expertise, confidence and experience. Some individuals and groups may find it difficult to take up an invitation to engage, or circumstances may prevent them from fully contributing to the engagement process. These resource and capacity issues need to be addressed to achieve the engagement purpose.

Profiling can help identify resource and capacity gaps. Never assume that there are common levels of knowledge and understanding. If there appear to be big gaps among stakeholders who are significantly impacted or who have a high level of impact, it may be worth going back to them and getting a fuller picture of their needs and to work together to understand and address these needs.

Areas where providing resources and building capacity may be relevant and beneficial include:

Knowledge

- understanding and awareness of the issues, the organisation, the local;

- culture and politics, related historic issues (need to be, and to be seen to be, even-handed here; sometimes multi-stakeholder groups commission their own experts to do this, so that no-one can say the expert is in the pay of any one party);

- knowledge of relevant approaches to stakeholder engagement; and

- understanding of the stakeholders involved and their perspectives.

Skills

- language, leadership and communication skills; and

- ability to examine and interpret the outputs of stakeholder engagement in a way that captures the key facts and figures, as well as messages and insights.

Resources

- availability of necessary financial and physical resources;

- availability of time to participate; and

- access to information in a timely and appropriate fashion.

When providing resources and building capacity it is important to:

- create a level playing field: work to ensure everybody involved understands the issues at stake;

- provide enough time: stakeholders require time to understand new information and form opinions; they also need time to build enough trust to engage; and

- be fair: when providing financial, or other, support to stakeholders, do so on the basis of clear eligibility criteria and in a transparent manner.

Case study 12: Natural resource company

To responsibly prepare for engagement in an effective manner a company working in natural resource exploitation in Europe undertook a series of pilot engagement projects. They first created a multi-stakeholder forum for community dialogue on local development support in a number of communities where they had operated for years but who, more and more, questioned and challenged their social responsibility. During this period, they also built internal capacity for engagement, and created an Engagement Management Procedure to:

- provide a corporate framework for stakeholder-related business and project risk management;

- help build partnerships to harness opportunities to jointly meet business and community goals;

- meet best practice in business development in support of their and their stakeholders' sustainable development;

- build their internal capacity to effectively use their community investment programs.

Three years later, recognising the value of engagement, the company set about integrating engagement into its core business through an overarching sustainability strategy – created to achieve profitable growth while acting sustainably and responsibly.

CHAPTER 6

How To Engage

THIS CHAPTER LOOKS AT HOW to successfully engage. It is essentially about the management system we use for the engagement process. As you see in the figure below, the management systems model we use is straightforward and based on the old Deming model of plan–do–check–act; or in this case: plan; implement; monitor and evaluate; and act, report and improve.

FIGURE 10. The Smart Engagement management system.

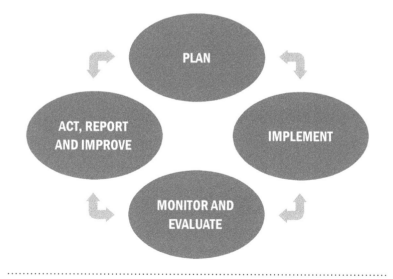

The key elements of each of these are:

Plan

- Clarify the purpose, scope and stakeholders (see the 'Why', the 'What' and the 'Who').

- Establish roles and relationships (see the 'Who').

- Establish principles and commitments.

- Profile, map and prioritise material issues and their stakeholders.

- Identify and prepare for engagement risks and opportunities.

- Determine the level and methods.

- Determine where and when.

Implement

- Mobilise resources.

- Build capacity (see the 'Who').

- Invite stakeholders to participate.

- Brief stakeholders.

- Engage.

- Develop an action plan.

Monitor and evaluate

- Develop indicators.

- Monitor and document.

- Evaluate.

Act, report and improve

- Act on action plan.

- Communicate decisions, action plan, actions and outputs to stakeholders.

- Report on engagement externally.

- Improve.

Plan

Before starting this section, let us stress that despite the focus on process, *Smart Engagement* is as much about mindset as it is about systems. Transparent planning processes are needed but only to the extent that they help focus our minds on what we need to achieve.

In this light, planning needs to be:

- **Outcome focused**: the engagement must help achieve the purpose of engagement;

- **Informed**: the engagement needs to be designed around a clear understanding of the purpose and scope; this requires a full understanding of all associated subject matter including the cultural and historical context;

- **Realistic**: all stakeholders need to have the required capacity and resources to engage;

- **Continually reviewed and improved**: maintain a spirit of continual improvement and accountability and act, review and report as you would in any other project management process.

The implementers of the engagement should put together an engagement plan. It should suit the scale of the engagement. A large, well-resourced engagement may require a full-scale formalised and approved plan. A small engagement should cover the basics and should be recorded so that you can review and improve at the end of the process. It is sometimes easiest to use a template for planning. You then know you have covered all the bases and all you have to do is fill in the blanks. You can develop your own planning headings and template to suit your circumstances.

Go to worksheet 6: Engagement plan –
www.smartbusinessacademy.org

Establish principles and commitments

Some principles

Principles are useful because they represent the underlying values that provide the foundation for what you are doing. They give you something to test your actions and decisions against. Have I taken the long view here? Have I been transparent? Am I being responsive?

The principles here are ones that we use and that work for us. They are not carved in stone. They have not been developed through an international consensus development process (although we look at all of those sets of principles and borrow what we like). The point is that it helps to have a set of principles or values that guide your actions – but you should feel free to adapt these principles if it makes engagement better.

Take the long view: Establishing and maintaining relationships requires a long-term view. This means:

- Invest in stakeholder relationships and engagement capacity, expectation management and following through on commitments.

- Invest in communication channels that are accessible and welcomed by stakeholders.

- Be a fair and committed partner.

- Take grievances and their resolution seriously.

Keep it simple: The whole purpose is to create value in a way that is technically feasible, economically viable and socially and environmentally acceptable. Complexity eats up time and other resources and often draws you down into the weeds and away from the purpose and desired outcomes.

Focus on what's important: Many people refer to this as focusing on what's material. The main point is 'don't sweat the small stuff'. Don't ignore it. Send it to housekeeping if it needs doing. But engagement should be about the important stuff. Don't leave out significant issues. These are the things that can help you create value or undermine your ability to create value. You don't need to engage on whether to use a 3-inch screw or a 3¼-inch screw: just do it.

Integrate: There are two meanings here. The first is that engagement must be integrated with core organisational functions. It is not something you do just to keep civil society off your back or tick a box to get financing approved. The second meaning has to do with the outcomes and the value engagement helps to create. For *Smart Engagement*, those outcomes and those values must be based on an integrated view of value. We don't want to sound like a broken record, but the value engagement can help us create and maintain is value that is technically feasible, economically viable and socially and environmentally acceptable. This means that we have to understand how those things are interconnected and interdependent.

Be inclusive: Social inclusion is a key aspect of *Smart Engagement*. It is worth repeating and emphasising. It is about ensuring that you are including all relevant voices in the decision-making process, and not taking other people's decisions without them. It means being actively and not passively inclusive.

Be responsive: If you are going to be inclusive you had better be responsive. Being responsive is about meeting and being responsive to expectations. Don't create expectations by engaging with somebody and listening to their views and concerns and then doing nothing. You can turn supporters into adversaries very quickly. If you get some input, respond to it. You can say yes, maybe or no, but you have to respond. When you respond it is advisable to justify your response – be accountable.

Be transparent: *Smart Business* is built on transparent practices and accountability. This increases understanding about your company and your activities, enables timely feedback and, when all material issues are addressed, leads to public trust and credibility. Be transparent in a complete and balanced way. Tell the good with the bad.

Some commitments
We've mentioned this before. *Smart Engagement* will fail without the necessary commitment from the highest levels.

- Management and the board must acknowledge that organisational success is closely linked with all stakeholders and commit to engagement as a core function.

- Management and the board must acknowledge the rightful owners of decisions and institutionalise an organisational culture that ensures decisions will be taken by those who own them.

- The organisation must systematically identify all stakeholders and go out of its way to build trust, enable constructive dialogue and identify areas of concern and common interests and values in a timely fashion.

- The organisations must commit to mobilising the required resources and sharing relevant information in a timely fashion.

Identify and prepare for engagement risks and opportunities

Engaging with stakeholders is not always easy. They can resist engagement for a wide range of reasons:

- previous bad experiences with your organisation or with the issues you are engaging on;

- lack of trust in your willingness to engage in good faith;

- fear of losing their position of power or of being perceived as co-opted;

- private interests that motivate them to see the engagement fail;

- lack of faith that engaging will make a difference to the outcome;

- lack of time, energy and resources.

As you develop your plan, make sure that you identify and plan responses to potential engagement risks. These can be numerous and unexpected if you haven't profiled your stakeholders well and prepared for all eventualities. Common engagement risks include:

- conflicts, or potential conflicts, between stakeholders who derail the agenda;

- disruptive stakeholders who interrupt constantly to drive a personal agenda;

- assertive stakeholders who dominate the discussion and make it difficult for less assertive stakeholders to participate; weak or marginalised stakeholders may have very valuable input to offer and the process must ensure balanced input;

- poorly prepared briefing material, non-credible briefing material, briefing material that lacks coverage of significant material issues;

- uninformed stakeholders who haven't read, listened to, or understood the briefing materials and take up too much time going over ground already covered;

- uncooperative stakeholders who've heard it all before, seen no action and cast a cynical pall over proceedings;

- internal stakeholders won't take it seriously and will undermine it;

- stakeholders unwilling to engage: you simply can't get anybody to respond to your questionnaire or come to your stakeholder forum.

Developing responses to these resistant stakeholders and stakeholder risks will often mean choosing levels and methods of engagement that are far from ideal. Engagement at an advanced level may not always be possible with high priority stakeholders. But it may still be possible to keep stakeholders fully and transparently informed. In engagement events or processes (e.g. a multi-stakeholder forum) it is important to ensure that the views of key stakeholders unwilling to engage are included in the discussion and dialogue. You need to keep the relationship open and, over time, work to move the relationship along from one engagement level to another. It is important to be aware that ignoring priority stakeholders is rarely a sustainable solution.

Determine the levels and methods

The level of engagement has to do with how close stakeholders are to collaborating on decision-making. This will depend on a number of factors:

- **The level of trust** between the organisation and its stakeholders – if there is little trust you will start at a lower level and move up the levels as you build trust;

- **The maturity of the relationship** with stakeholders – if you or your stakeholders are new to engagement you will start at a lower level and move up the levels as you build your understanding of each other;

- **The capacity of the organisation and its stakeholders** – they should have the aptitudes, skills and knowledge needed to participate effectively at the chosen level; if they don't, you may need to engage at a lower level until you build capacity to engage at a higher level;

- **The openness** of the organisation **to shared decision-making** (where legally possible) – there is no use engaging at a high level, where the expectation is shared decision-making, if the organisation will go ahead and make decisions unilaterally anyway: this will only lead to frustration and undermine trust;

- **The relative importance of the purpose** of the engagement – while engagement should always focus on the most important issues, some are more important than others and not all warrant the resource commitment of a high level of engagement;

- **The urgency of the issue** – you may need to address a challenge very quickly; this may not allow the time needed for a high level of engagement (unless you have a standing stakeholder engagement forum that you can quickly convene), so you may have to engage at a lower level quickly and then revisit the issue at a higher level when time allows; and

- **The influence of stakeholders** – you may be in a position where you are under pressure from stakeholders who have a high level of influence in the marketplace or with other stakeholders; because of their influence these stakeholders will want and need to be taken seriously and will not settle for a low level of engagement.

There is a wide range of methods and techniques to choose from at each engagement level. Choosing the methods, techniques and tools that will work best depends on a number of factors.

- **The relationships between stakeholders** – if there are tensions between stakeholders it may be best to engage one-on-one or in small groups rather that in a multi-stakeholder forum;

- **The resources available** – if there are limited resources it may be better to use social media than convening a face-to-face forum; and

- **The types of outputs you are looking for** – you will use different techniques to brainstorm than to build consensus.

Choosing the correct combination of levels and methods for each engagement is crucial for its success.

We differentiate between 'pre-engagement' levels and methods and 'engagement' levels and methods. Engagement implies dialogue. A lot of what is called engagement is one-sided. It is these necessary but one-sided activities that we call pre-engagement. We identify two pre-engagement levels: tracking and informing. We identify four engagement levels: consulting, including, collaborating and empowering. As you move higher up the levels, engagement will have higher impact but may also require greater input in time and resources.

FIGURE 11. Levels and example methods of engagement.

HOW? Levels and methods

Increasing time and resources required

Level	Pre-engagement		Engagement			
Methods	**Track**	**Inform**	**Consult**	**Involve**	**Collaborate**	**Empower**
	Proactively listen	Leaflets	Surveys	One-on-one discussions	Joint projects	Delegated decisions
	Media watch	Newsletters	Polling	Group discussions	Partnerships	Integration of stake-holders into governance
	Unsolicited correspondence	Reports	Focus groups	Multi-stakeholder forums	Participatory decision-making	
	Complaints	Speeches	Feedback sessions	Advisory panels	Consensus building forums	
	Claims	Presentations	Meetings and workshops			
	Protests	Press releases	Public meetings			
	Websites	Websites	Public comment periods			
	Social networks	Advertisements				
		Open houses				

90

The higher levels of engagement build on the lower levels. Stakeholders will not feel ready to make an empowered decision if they do not feel appropriately informed, consulted, involved and collaborated with. In many situations, moving up from one level to the next is a voluntary process: all stakeholders need to be informed, those who want to be consulted should be consulted, those who want to be involved should be given the opportunity to be involved and so on.

Case study 13: Large manufacturing plant

A large manufacturing plant was closed following a decision that the costs to make it compliant with environmental standards while at the same time compete on the global market were too high. When deliberating what to do to address responsibly the challenges raised by this decision, it became apparent that the affected communities should be engaged. The first step was to rebuild trust. The company believed that the community would disrupt the process. The community believed that the organisation would not be interested in their opinions. It took one year to rebuild trust. This was achieved through cooperation on various community development initiatives led by the community and supported by the company and the local authorities.

The engagement started with a series of one-to-one and small group meetings to understand the current situation. This was followed by an open invitation to participate in information exchanges on community development challenges that eventually developed into a series of community projects developed through mini-grants that covered material costs, and partnerships that covered management and implementation.

The relationships matured and engagement moved up to a level where a multi-stakeholder forum was possible. Once its membership grew to a critical mass, participants elected their own council members and the company and the local authorities appointed their own. Meaningful discussions started on the most appropriate steps to be taken to address the challenges imposed by the closure of the plant. All council meetings were recorded and relayed back to stakeholders for input and feedback.

Where and when

When: There are at least five things that influence when you should engage:

- the urgency of the need for engagement (how soon do you need a decision?);

- the capacity to plan and implement on time (you need a decision quickly but you want to do a proper job and not set yourself up for failure);

- the availability of resources (if the budget is not there this quarter you are just going to have to wait – either that or find the resources);

- the calendar (e.g. the three weeks before and after Christmas are not a good time; August in France is not a good time);

- the availability of key stakeholders (you will have to adjust to their schedules); and

- stakeholder fatigue (you have invited some of these people to five events in the last ten months – they don't work for you).

Where: When considering where to engage, the best option is to engage stakeholders on their home ground or on neutral territory. This could be electronically. The benefits of this are as follows:

- it is respectful and so will enable a more productive engagement process;

- it contributes to stakeholders' sense of ownership over the engagement process;

- it increases the transparency of the process – they talk about matters that they can see;

- it increases the accountability of local leaders through key discussions and communication on bilateral issues being done in the open and not behind closed doors;

- it enables a genuine internal–external stakeholder team building.

Where it is not possible to engage locally, the engagement should take place at a mutually agreed location. Additionally, the engagement activities should be appropriate for the context and agreed with by the stakeholders.

Implement

Mobilise resources

Resources are required for the engagement itself, but organisations often forget that they will also need resources to make the changes required by the outputs of engagement.

To come up with a reasonable sense of what resources you will need you should look at the engagement plan. The resources will include:

- financial resources;

- human resources (including capacity building);

- technological resources.

Resources will be needed both for those carrying out the engagement and for the stakeholders invited to participate.

Stakeholders may wish or need to be compensated for their time as well as for expenses incurred in order to participate in the engagement. Any financial support should be designed in such a way that it does not represent a potential for conflict of interest.

The engagement should not proceed if the necessary resources are not provided.

Invite stakeholders to participate

Some engagement methods don't require an invitation. You can simply send out a survey or provide a mechanism for public comments. But most methods where there is any face-to-face contact will require an invitation. Any invitation you send out should provide enough information for potential participants to make a reasonably informed decision about whether to accept or not. This might include:

- the purpose and scope of the engagement;

- the engagement process and timelines;

- what stakeholders are expected to contribute;

- the benefits to the stakeholder invited to participate;

- logistical and practical information about the engagement;

- a query about accessibility needs;

- how to respond;

- additional information that will be provided; and

- next steps.

Invitations should always be personal. Send them to a real person not to 'the occupant' or 'to whom it may concern'. If you haven't invited the right person, then ask whoever you did invite to let you know who the right person is. But really you should have done all of this when you were doing the stakeholder profiling.

Invitations don't have to be on engraved cards. Use a method appropriate to the method of engagement. Consider using snail mail, email, messages via social networks, telephone calls and personal visits. You should also follow up. Make sure they got the invitation and then confirm whether they will participate. If the invitation has gone out well in advance you may want to schedule periodic follow ups to make sure they don't forget.

Brief stakeholders

Briefing materials help make sure everybody comes prepared and ready to engage on a level playing field. Send them out in advance – not so far in advance that they get put in the 'to do' file, forgotten and don't get read or viewed but also not so late that the participants don't have enough time to go over them. Five to ten days in advance is good. These briefing materials should cover:

- how the issues are currently managed within the organisation;

- what policies and systems are already in place;

- a review of all relevant subject matter, including cultural and historical context; and

- options already being considered.

In some cases, especially where you have been building capacity, it may be helpful to have pre-meetings, informal conversations, or to hold training or briefing sessions.

Materials should be easy to understand, clearly highlight the key points and should take into account any relevant language, disability and literacy issues.

You should also give participants the opportunity to prepare and circulate briefing materials.

Case study 14: Public utility

A large public utility had a standing stakeholder panel for environmental issues. Many members had been on the panel for three years or more. Early in the panel's history the panel's secretariat prepared and circulated briefing materials in advance

---

of every meeting. This seemed to work well. People came prepared and the engagements were fruitful.

After a couple of years the briefing materials started to get longer and more detailed. It was becoming clear that members were no longer always reading all of the materials and the productivity and value of the panel decreased. There was information overload.

The panel discussed the situation and came up with the following changes.

Briefing materials would not be sent out in bulk all at once 10 days before each meeting. Instead, an intranet for the panel would be set up. Materials would be uploaded when prepared and members would be sent emails notifying them of the new materials.

1. The main entry for each briefing would only be a summary of key points. There would then be a link to more detailed materials for those who wanted to know more.

2. Members could upload their own briefing materials or request briefing materials online.

3. Members could comment online on the materials that had been uploaded.

The result was a return to productivity of the panel.

Engage

To engage effectively you need some ground rules. Here are some that we have used. Experiment with these and develop your own. It can also be useful to start a session by asking stakeholders to collaborate in the selection, development or validation of the ground rules.

- Don't assign intentions, beliefs or motives to others. Ask others questions instead of stating untested assumptions about them.

- Honour everyone's right to 'pass' if they are not ready or willing to speak.

- Allow others to express their opinions completely.

- Give everyone the opportunity to speak.

- Respect confidentiality or anonymity requests where possible.

- Be solutions-oriented.

- Stay focused on the issue.

During the engagement, as a result of stakeholder input, it may be appropriate to revise the purpose and scope of the engagement. During the engagement be watchful for and immediately identify and address any potential issues, for example:

- distrust;

- intimidation;

- rivalries between individuals and organisations;

- poorly defined issues or problems;

- emotionally upsetting situations;

- unhelpful complexity;

- unhelpful digression;

- unbalanced participation; or

- poor time utilisation.

Finally, make sure all views, key points, action items and decisions are captured. If you want to make audio, video or photographic records make sure all participants agree. If there are any Freedom of Information requirements – make sure all participants are aware of these from the outset.

Develop an action plan

Having recorded all of the views, key points, action items and decisions from the engagement, you now need to turn these into an action plan for those who need to do something. The action plan is not necessarily only for the organisation at the heart of the engagement. Stakeholders may have decided that others also need to act. For example, they may have recommendations for local government, for research bodies or for community groups. The point is to make sure that the outputs of the engagement are made concrete and communicated to those who need to act.

Monitor and evaluate

Develop indicators

The first thing you need to do to monitor and evaluate is to select or develop a set of indicators. Indicators allow you to measure and evaluate how well you are doing and what you have achieved. You need indicators in four areas:

1. engagement management;

2. engagement quality;

3. eerformance against outputs; and

4. eerformance against outcomes.

It generally takes a lot of shared experience between stakeholders before a mutually agreed set of indicators that clearly demonstrate the value of the engagement can be generated. Key Performance Indicators (KPIs), therefore, need to be developed iteratively over time. It is always helpful to start with a set of KPIs developed through dialogue with all stakeholders.

Internally, for engagement management you may want to have indicators for:

- response or participation rates; and

- performance against plan – on time, on budget.

Measuring aspects of engagement quality is a matter of connecting pieces of information and being alert to signals that identify changes in perceptions and emerging patterns, and designing a process to monitor these. This can often be done through exit interviews or questionnaires at the end of meetings, or follow-up perception surveys. You may seek to monitor such aspects as:

- Were the right people involved?

- Was the engagement level and method appropriate?

- Was the engagement well managed/facilitated?

- Did the engagement produce useful and credible outputs?

Also, throughout the engagement there needs to be a clear mechanism for stakeholders to express grievances so that the engagement can focus on constructive dialogue and grievances are addressed quickly and correctly.

For outputs, you really need to measure whether or not they were acted on and what the results (outcomes) were. This will require some generic indicators and then some indicators specific to the decision or action. You may want to assess:

- Did the action plan include all engagement outputs?

- Did the organisation provide a credible response to all outputs?

- What decisions and actions were implemented?

- How did the organisation perform in relation to implemented decisions and actions?

Evaluating outcomes requires us to think about value. What we want to know is what value was created or protected as a result of the decisions and actions taken in response to the engagement. The indicators you select will be specific to the outcomes you set out to achieve. Since *Smart Engagement* is designed to generate technically feasible, economically viable, and socially and environmentally acceptable outcomes, the best way to do this is to select or develop indicators that monitor and evaluate the value created in these areas.

As with any other monitoring and evaluation process you should write a monitoring and evaluation (M&E) plan (keep it simple) and draw up a list of indicators you will use. For each indicator you should have a supporting page that describes why you chose it, what it means, how to collect the data, who will collect the data, how to compile and evaluate the data, who needs to see the data and so on.

TABLE 2. Sample indicator chart

Engagement management	Engagement quality	Performance against outputs	Performance against outcomes
Response or participation rates	Were the right people involved?	Did the action plan include all engagement outputs?	Technically feasible
Performance against plan – on time, on budget	Was the engagement level and method appropriate?	Did the organisation provide a credible response to all outputs?	Economically viable
	Was the engagement well managed/facilitated?	What decisions and actions were implemented?	Socially acceptable and sustainable
	Did the engagement produce useful and credible outputs?	How did the organisation perform in relation to implemented decisions and actions?	Environ-mentally acceptable and sustainable

Monitor and document

With your indicators in place you need a monitoring and evaluation plan in place to make sure the information is gathered, stored and distributed to the right people.

The M&E plan should include the following:

- a statement of purpose;

- a short description of the key inputs, activities, outcomes and outputs;

- a list of all associated indicators with supporting guidance (roles, collection etc.);

- a description of the data flow;

- a note on types and frequency of analysis; and

- a note on external verification and audit.

The plan should also cover internal reporting for management purposes and external reporting. Internal reporting, in addition to output and outcome data, will include information on the broader set of input and engagement process indicators. External reporting should focus on performance against output and outcome targets and the contribution of the engagement to the organisation's creation of value.

Evaluate

Evaluation is mostly a comparative exercise.

- You may want to understand how well you have done against your own targets.

- You may want to know how much you have improved year on year.

- You may want to know how well you are doing in relation to regional or sector benchmarks.

- You may want to know if you are contributing your fair or expected share to global or regional issues.

- You may want to know the return on investment of your engagement.

You may want to know all kinds of things. The trick is to find the stories in the data. But if you have good indicators and good clean data you can get the stakeholders involved in analysing the data and finding the narrative.

Act, report and improve

Act on action plan

As we said earlier, you shouldn't engage if you are not going to act on the outputs of the engagement. As we also said, when you are considering the resources needed for engagement you should also consider the resources that might be required to act on the outputs.

So if you have read this far, you have no excuse now for not acting.

Communicate decisions, action plan, actions and outputs to stakeholders

Documents and records: To communicate effectively you need good documents and records. You should keep all relevant documents and records throughout the entire engagement process: planning;

implementation; monitoring and evaluation; act, review and improve.

Communications: You should communicate with the organisation and with engagement participants at all stages and in a timely manner. We recommend these basic best practice principles for communication and transparency.

- Disclose early: provide relevant information to stakeholders in advance of decision-making. At all times promote transparency and accountability in communication.

- Be credible: disclose objective information and refrain from exaggerating the positive aspects, while playing down the negative; keep actions ahead of words.

- Design disclosure to support consultation: give people the information they need to participate in an informed manner and allow sufficient time in between disclosure and consultation.

- Provide accessible information: in a language that is readily understandable, tailored to the target stakeholders (language, culture, social sensitivities) and is in a format they find attractive.

- Have it reviewed by stakeholders: tends to be more accessible and credible.

- Provide feedback loops: to gauge to what extent communication goals were achieved.

There are a number of key internal reporting points.

- Implementers of the engagement reporting to the organisation and participants on the running and outputs of the engagement.

- Implementers of the engagement reporting to the organisation and participants on the proposed action plan resulting from the outputs of the engagement.

- The initiators and others required to take action reporting to the participants in the engagement on their response to the action plan.

- The initiators and others required to take action reporting periodically to the participants in the engagement on performance against decisions and actions.

- The initiators and others required to take action reporting periodically to the participants on performance against outcomes associated with the purpose of the engagement.

Report on engagement externally

Integrated and sustainability reporting guidelines (e.g. IIRC and GRI) now require organisations to report on stakeholder engagement practices. While the reporting requirements are not particularly onerous they are a start. We would like to see organisations report more fully on their engagement practices. Having good M&E systems and indicators in place will help this.

It would be nice to see organisations reporting not only on their engagement management practices and the quality of their engagement but also on their performance against engagement outputs and outcomes. And perhaps even on the value created as a result of engagement and the return on investment of engagement.

Improve

This is all about learning from experience. We would suggest a few simple steps.

1. Have a formal debrief. Set aside a half-day or more to review everything that happened.

2. Identify all points where you could have done better, both in the engagement process and in responding to and acting on the outputs. Record them.

3. Brainstorm ways to do it better for each point. Read new materials, new guidelines, new research. Agree on solutions. Record them.

4. Revise your procedures or systems and write everything down somewhere so that if you leave you don't take all of the learning with you and leave nothing behind.

Since the debriefing is also a sort of engagement, feel free to invite others to the debrief – perhaps a participant or two, perhaps somebody who was not part of the process but who knows about engagement and can bring a fresh perspective.

You don't have to wait for the engagement process to be completed to review it. Constantly review your current process and its components and be open to improve as you go.

Key Terms

Organisation[1]

An entity, group of people, company, corporation, firm, enterprise, site, authority or institution, or part or combination thereof, whether corporate, government or civil society, that has its own functions and administration.

Output

The immediate result of a decision or activity.

Outcome

The changes or benefits resulting from an output.

Smart outcome

Changes or benefits that meet the needs of society and the environment as well as of the organisation.

Smart business

A business that delivers results (or outcomes) that are not only financially and technically successful but also socially and environmentally acceptable and sustainable.

Stakeholder[2]

Stakeholders are those individuals, groups of individuals or organisations who:

- affect and/or could be affected by an organisation's activities, decisions, products or services and associated performance;

- may have knowledge of, an interest in, or views about an organisation;

- may have diverse and sometimes conflicting interests and concerns.

Stakeholder engagement
The process used by an organisation to engage relevant stakeholders for a purpose to achieve accepted outcomes.[3]

Smart engagement
Smart engagement is a stakeholder engagement process designed and implemented with stakeholders that results in accepted, accountable and sustainable outputs and outcomes.

Notes

1. AA1000SES (2011).

2. Adapted from AA1000SES (2011) and ISO26000 (2010).

3. AA1000SES (2011).

....

Further Reading

The AA1000SES (2011) – the international standard on stakeholder engagement (see **www.aa1000ses.net**).

www.iap2.org – includes useful practical guidance on engagement techniques and IAP2 practitioners' experience.

www.ifc.org/ifcext/enviro.nsf/Content/Publications_GoodPractice_ StakeholderEngagement – the IFC/World Bank stakeholder engagement guidelines.

www.commdev.org – a capacity-building platform for oil and gas companies working in partnership with communities they impact with case studies from the oil, gas and mining industries.

http://www.ifc.org/ifcext/sustainability.nsf/Content/Publications_ Handbook_CommunityInvestment – created in 2010 to help IFC client companies and the wider private sector to think strategically about how they can support community investment programs that are successful, sustainable, and consistent with their business objectives.

http://www.ipieca.org/publication/guide-successful-sustainable- social-investment-oil-and-gas-industry – created in 2008 by the oil and gas industry addressing the question of how to create successful and sustainable community investments and how to measure their success.

For Product Safety Concerns and Information please contact our EU
representative GPSR@taylorandfrancis.com
Taylor & Francis Verlag GmbH, Kaufingerstraße 24, 80331 München, Germany